THE BRAVEST ALPACA

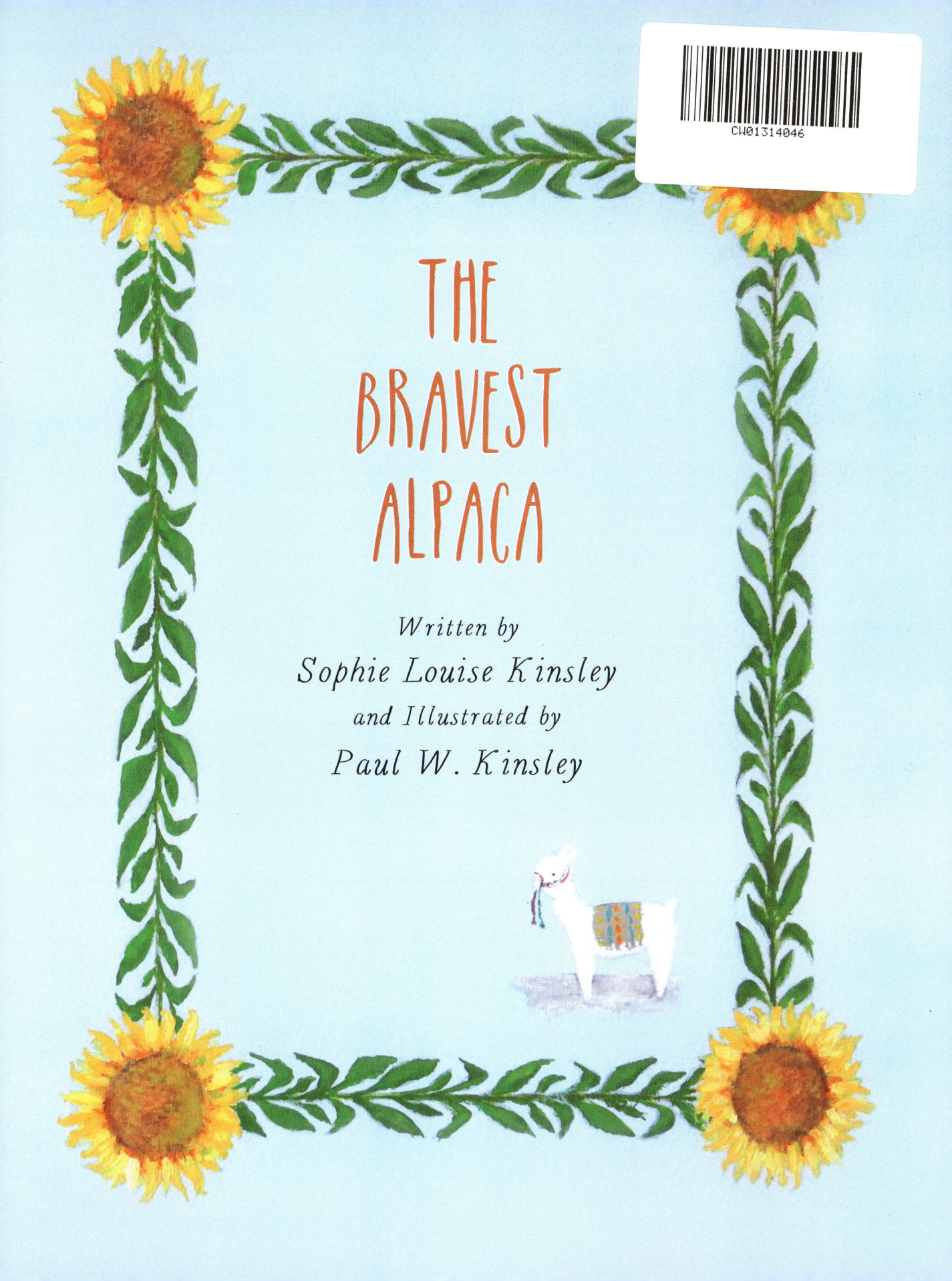

Written by
Sophie Louise Kinsley
and Illustrated by
Paul W. Kinsley

For most of my life that I could remember,
I had no name.

I AM A TINY ALPACA WHO ONCE LIVED IN A VILLAGE IN PERU

inside a large wicker basket with my many friends. We had been created by the villagers out of wool, beads and coloured thread and had been given the magical gift of coming to life, whenever there was no one around.

I had lived in the basket for years, as I was the smallest alpaca of them all and could hide very easily.

WE HAD BEEN MADE FOR TOURISTS

who wanted a reminder of their travels in Peru, and so far in my exciting life I had managed to hide at the bottom of the basket, because I never wanted to leave my friends.

My tiny alpaca friends and I played together

as soon as the sun dropped behind the hills of our village and everyone had gone to sleep. We couldn't wait to get out of our basket at night to run around chasing one another, playing, laughing and enjoying ourselves.

Before the sun rose in the morning, we made our way back into our basket, where we had to be very still and quiet during the day as there were always lots of people near.

One day, after a very happy night of high jinks, I was staring up at the searing sun when, without warning, a very pink,

ENORMOUS HAND RUSTLED AROUND IN MY BASKET AND GRABBED ME.

I could see the other miniature alpacas gasping as they looked up at me, and I wondered if I would ever see them again.

A lady with auburn hair paid some money to Beatriz, the lady who had made me,

AND BEFORE I KNEW IT I HAD BEEN PLACED CAREFULLY INSIDE HER RUCKSACK.

I felt very frightened and started looking around the inside of her bag for something that would reassure me, but all I could find was a pink woolly jumper (which didn't smell very nice at all), some sandwiches and a camera. I tucked myself in near the jumper, which was made of soft wool, and I felt comforted.

I SOON DISCOVERED THAT THE LADY WHO HAD PICKED ME WAS CALLED JANE,

and she was trekking with her friends from somewhere a long way from *my* home. I kept getting jostled around as she was walking and tried carefully to find my footing, but it was difficult to remain on all my toes when I couldn't see where we were going.

After a few hours of the group walking, talking and laughing, it felt like we were getting higher and higher into the hills until all of a sudden, we stopped. Jane sat down and put her rucksack on its side.

I STUMBLED BUT I COULD FINALLY SEE OUT!

I put my nose out of the rucksack and smelt the beautiful, clean, fresh air and saw the softest, greenest ground I had ever seen. I had never travelled this high or so far in my life, and I knew at once that this was Machu Picchu, an ancient fortress in the mountains that I could see from my village. My friends had talked about this magical place and suddenly I felt very excited that I could tell them all about my adventures when we went back home.

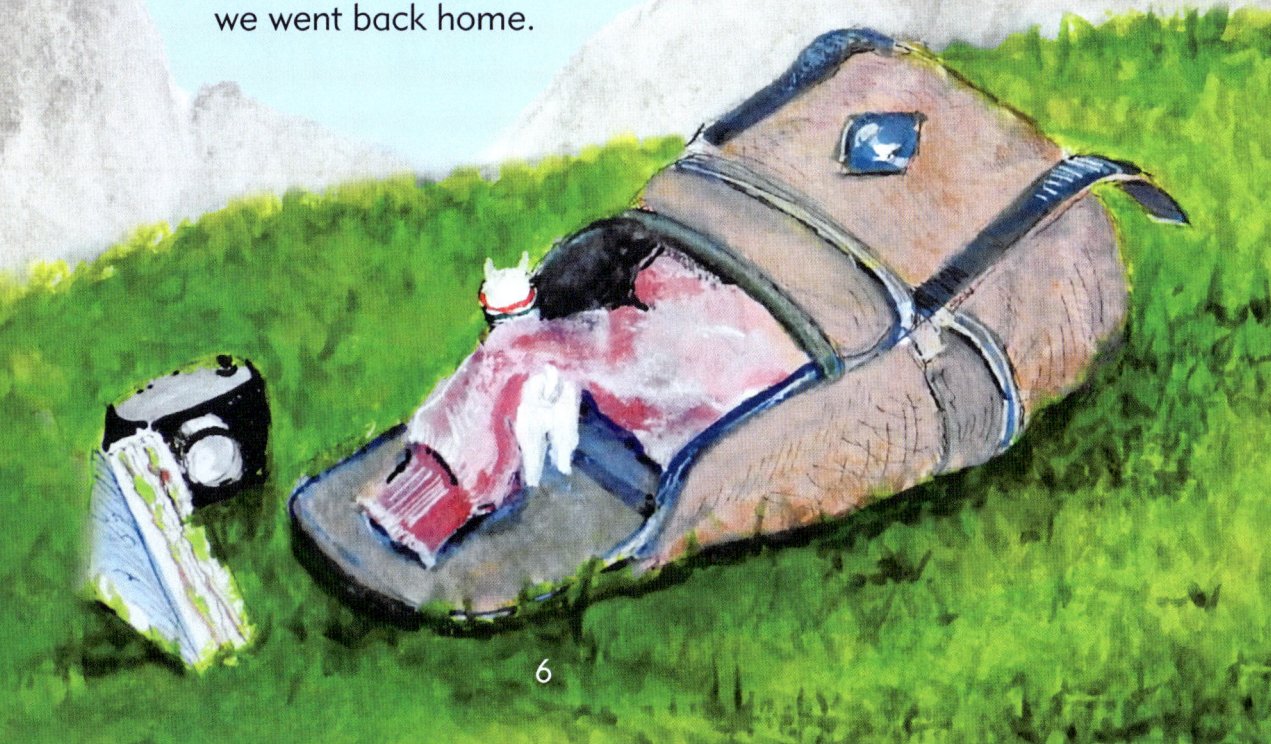

I stayed there with Jane and her friends for many more hours, and we watched the sun set before heading back down the mountain. I had never had a more adventurous day in my life.

IT WAS SO EXCITING!

Eventually we made our way to the bottom of the mountain, past the village where I came from and into a townhouse, or a 'hostel' as Jane called it. Jane told her friends that she was really tired, so she was going to go to bed early, as they were flying home tomorrow morning.

She took me out of her rucksack and gently placed me on her bedside table.

'OH, YOU ARE SO SWEET! I SHALL CALL YOU JEFF!'

And that is how I got my name; I am Jeff the miniature alpaca.

I wondered when Jane would remember to take me back to the village to see my friends, because I had to tell them all about my adventures and how I had visited Machu Picchu.

I SLEPT SOUNDLY THAT NIGHT.

I was tired from all the surprises that had happened and so I drifted off into a world full of beautiful dreams and sunshine.

Jane woke me up while it was still dark, and she seemed very frantic packing everything into her rucksack.

She glanced around the room as she was about to leave...

...and ran back to me.

'OH, JEFF, HOW COULD I FORGET YOU?'

She picked me up and put me into a side pocket of her rucksack, which was made of mesh so I had a good view of the outside.

BUT I FELT VERY AFRAID.

Jane met up with her friends who were all very noisy, even though it was the morning *and* still dark. They all jumped into a big car they called a taxi. I *had* seen cars before, as they had driven into our village, but she told the man driving the car that they wanted to go to the airport.

THE AIRPORT? WHAT DID SHE MEAN? I THOUGHT JANE WAS GOING TO TAKE ME HOME FIRST?

I felt my bottom lip quiver and I tried to be brave, but I felt some tears roll down my face and onto my fur. She must have forgotten about taking me back home to my village.

I FELT MY HEART SINK WITH A SADNESS I HAD NEVER FELT BEFORE.

All of the bags and rucksacks had been put into the back of the car and a lid had shut.

IT WAS SO DARK,

but not the kind of darkness I knew from night-time, when we always had the light from the moon to see by.

I think I must have been in there for many hours before the car stopped and the lid opened to let in the light. I could see the driver peering in at me. Jane and her friends were there too, talking to one another.

'Alright in there, Jeff?', she laughed. She picked up her rucksack with me in it and put it on her back.

'WE'VE GOT TO GO!',

called out one of her friends. 'We're running late and don't want to miss our flight.'

It took me some time to adjust my eyes to the brightness of the sunlight and I hung on tightly to the mesh of the rucksack as Jane and her friends ran into the airport.

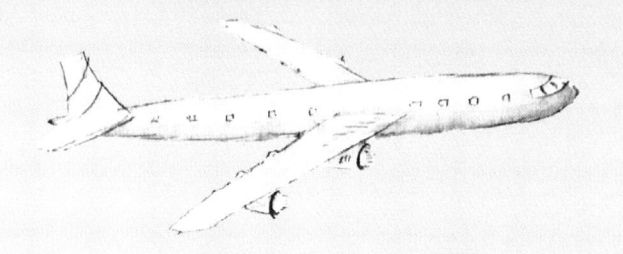

I had never known such a commotion. There was so much going on, hundreds of people all looking so busy, all in a hurry to get somewhere. It was all very overwhelming and I longed to be back in the village with my friends.

Everyone was handing over their luggage to very official looking people in uniforms, and I was concerned that I would be separated from Jane. She was just going to hand over her rucksack to a man in a uniform when she said, 'Jeff, where's Jeff?' She reached into the side pocket of her rucksack to pick me up, and put me straight into her handbag.

'YOU'RE NOT GOING IN THE HOLD WITH THE REST OF THE LUGGAGE. YOU'RE COMING WITH ME, LITTLE FELLOW!'

Jane smiled as she was talking to me and I could see that she had the kindest of faces.

Her handbag was full of all sorts of things: a lipstick, handkerchiefs, a chocolate bar, a phone and a passport. The passport at the top had made a shape like a teepee, so I quickly darted underneath it for shelter.

I WAS SHAKING WITH WORRY AS TO WHAT COULD POSSIBLY HAPPEN NEXT.

Jane's friends were getting impatient waiting for her.

'I had to get Jeff out', she shouted over to them.

'Who is Jeff?' one of the ladies called Bella asked.

'Jeff. You know who Jeff is! He's the little wool alpaca I bought yesterday as a souvenir, from our trek to Machu Picchu.'

I didn't know what a souvenir was but it sounded very grand and I felt quite pleased with myself that I was a 'soo-ven-ear'.

Bella called over, 'Oh Jane, he's not real! I can't believe you've named him!'

Jane got me out and put me in the palms of her hands and looked me straight in the eye.

'YOU ARE REAL, AREN'T YOU, JEFF?'

and at that very moment it was all I could do to hold back from nodding and replying,

'YES, I AM AS REAL AS YOU ARE, JANE.'

We heard someone announce in a very loud voice, 'Could all passengers get ready to board for London.'

'Ooh, that's us', said Jane, excitedly.

'Phew, we just made it', muttered Bella.

Jane couldn't possibly mean 'us' as in her friends and me. How could we be going to London? Did she mean London in England? My home is in Peru, in the village. I don't want to go to London. It's cold and it rains and the river is brown.

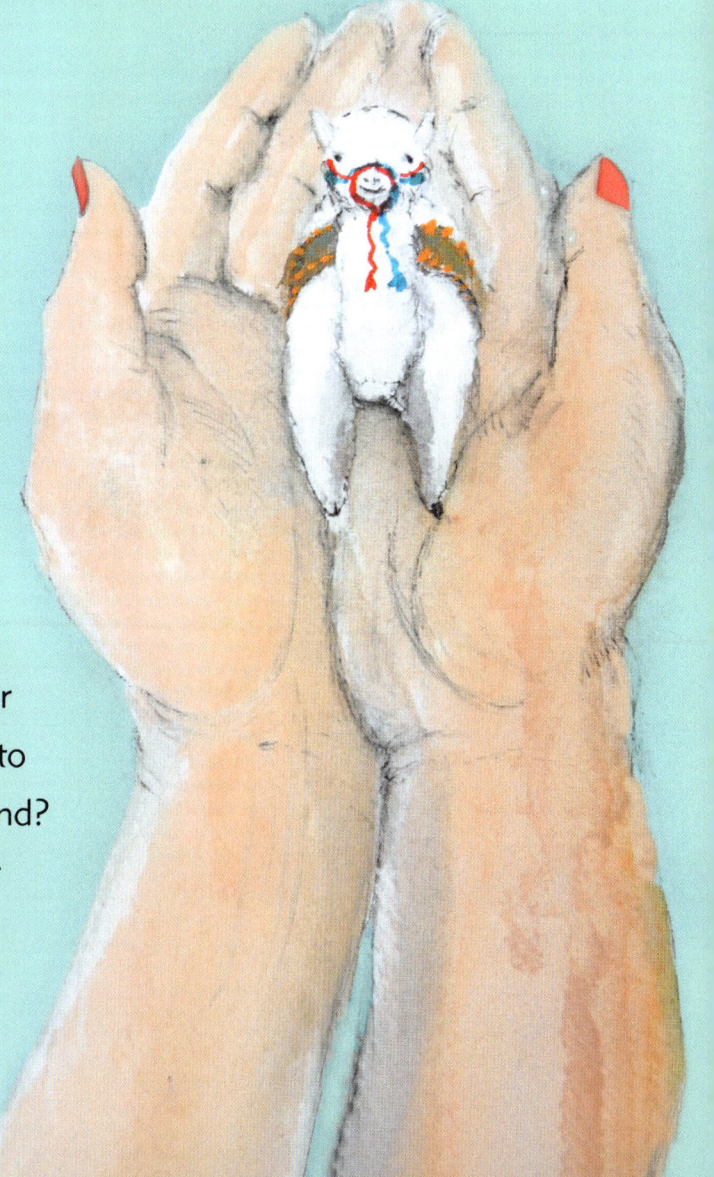

I had no time to think, and before I knew it Jane was finding her seat on this huge contraption called an aeroplane. I had seen an aeroplane before, but I thought it was just a funny-shaped bird that made lots of noise when it flew across the sky. She said to me,

'THIS IS GOING TO BE YOUR FIRST FLIGHT, JEFF, SO YOU HAVE TO BE BRAVE.'

I felt as if I had been nothing *but* brave ever since Jane had set eyes on me!

Our plane got ready for take-off and it was the loudest noise I had ever heard. Louder than being in the car or coming to the airport, with all the hustle and bustle. After a few hours of being in the sky, I realised Jane and her friends had fallen asleep, so I very carefully looked out from underneath the passport.

MY GOODNESS, WHAT A SHOCK!

There must have been hundreds of people on the plane. Some people were sound asleep, others wide awake, and some people were looking as scared as I felt. I couldn't believe we were so high up in the sky. All I could see were white fluffy clouds, and it was hard to see what was below us. At times I wasn't sure if this was actually a dream or really happening.

Eventually I fell asleep on the plane, into the deepest of sleeps. When I woke up, our plane had landed on a cold and wet concrete landscape. I shivered and wrapped a cotton handkerchief around me to keep warm.

Jane called out, 'It's freezing cold. Let's go back to South America', and all of her friends laughed.

DID SHE REALLY MEAN IT? CAN WE POSSIBLY GO BACK HOME?

Jane whispered into her handbag to me, 'This is the London airport, Jeff. Hold tight and we will be home soon.'

It took us two hours in a car before we finally got home to Jane's house in a seaside town, where the sun had just started to shine. By now she had said goodbye to all of her friends and it was just the two of us. Jane thanked the man who had driven us and she carried her rucksack to the door of her house.

It was cold inside her house and she grumbled about it. She dropped her rucksack on the floor and rooted around in her handbag for her phone, narrowly missing grabbing my tail in the process. She then telephoned her Mum and Dad to tell them she was safely back home.

I started to wonder if she had forgotten about me and it was starting to get a little bit uncomfortable in her handbag.

'JEFF! OH, YOU POOR THING, COME HERE! LET'S MAKE YOU FEEL AT HOME NOW.'

She placed me on her sofa and went upstairs. I could see that Jane had a camel made of felt on her mantelpiece. I smiled at the camel and he winked at me.

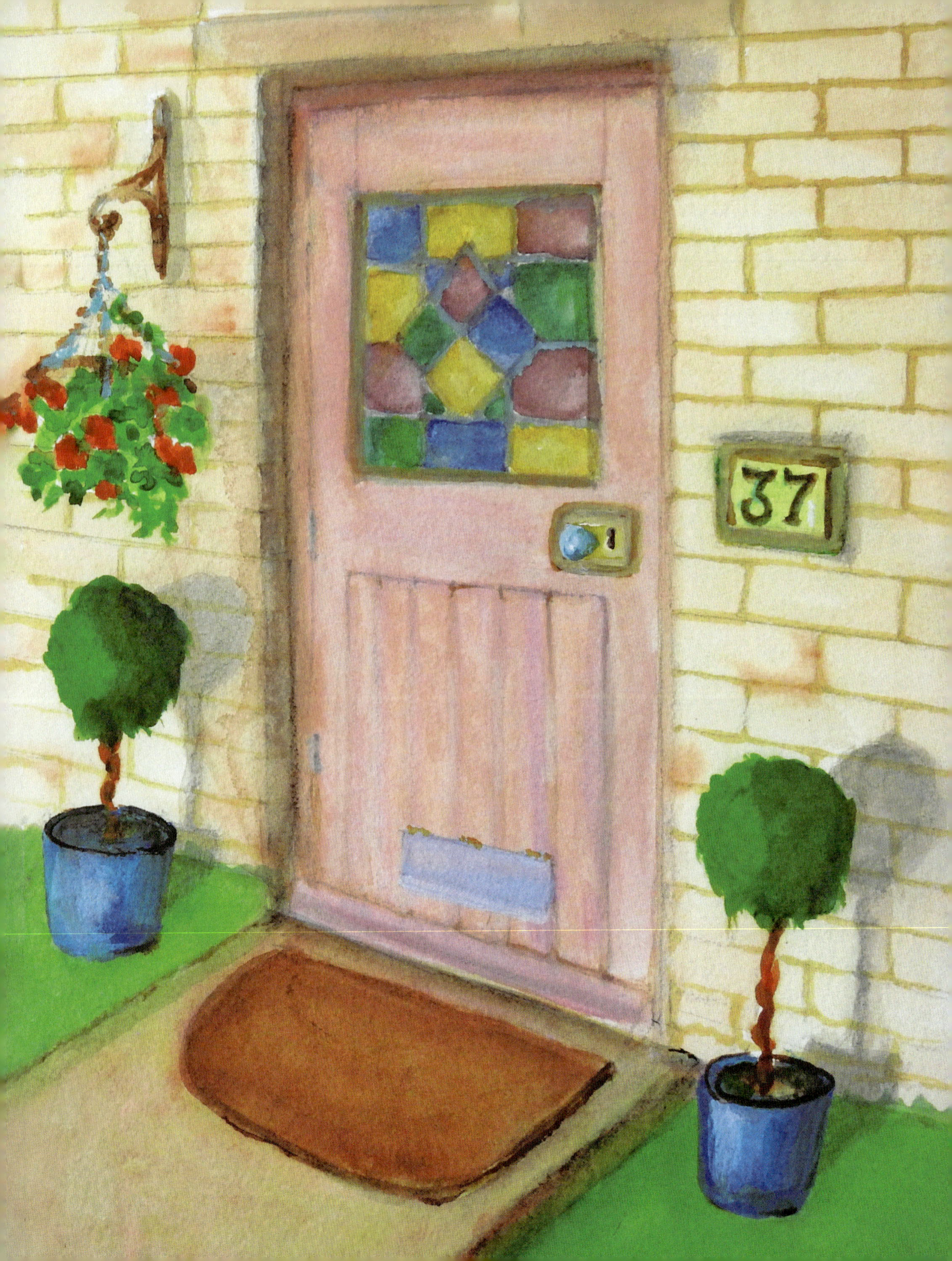
37

OH GOODNESS ME, A FRIEND I CAN TALK TO. HOW EXCITING!

Jane came back downstairs and said to me, 'Do you want to stand next to Norman on the mantelpiece?' She picked me up and put me next to the camel, who was a lot bigger than I was.

'OH, DON'T YOU TWO LOOK THE PART! YOU REALLY ARE THE BRAVEST ALPACA I HAVE EVER MET!'

She stepped back to admire us both, smiling.

'Got to go to bed boys, as I need to unpack and then go to sleep. So make friends and get to know one another. Be nice!'

And with that she turned the light off and left the door slightly ajar, letting in the light from the staircase.

I FELT NORMAN LOOKING AT ME OUT OF THE CORNER OF HIS EYE.

'SO, YOU'RE CALLED JEFF THEN?'

'Me?'

'Who else?' he said abruptly.

I felt very small and quite upset that he had snapped at me but I remembered Jane telling me to be brave.

'Yes, my name is Jeff and I have come from Peru. I'm hoping that I can get back to my friends in the village soon.'

'Oh, don't be so silly', said Norman. 'You can't go back there. *This* is your home now and you've got to make the most of it.'

'But I thought I was going to go back home and that maybe this is a holiday.'

'NO, NO, NO! YOUR HERE TO STAY, BOY.'

Oh my goodness! My friends, the sunshine, the village… The sadness and longing for what I once knew was overwhelming, but I had to keep being brave.

'IF I CAN'T GO BACK HOME, NORMAN, WILL *YOU* BE MY FRIEND?'

Norman paused and let out a big sigh.

'Well if I have to be', he retorted. He started moving his lips from side to side as if he was chewing on something.

I smiled at him and he put his nose in the air, carried on chewing and looked the other way.

It was hard to tell if he liked me or not. He was one of those camels that seemed very confident and a little bit rude at times.

I had met a few alpacas like Norman before and I found that they were never ever as frosty as they pretended to be, once I showed them my kindness and good heart.

'Where have you come from Norman?', I asked.

'My dear, innocent young alpaca! Well I'm not from the North Pole, that's for certain. I come from Egypt. I was created near the Great Pyramids and, quite honestly, that is where highly cultured, intelligent camels belong.'

'BUT HOW DID YOU END UP HERE...

...ON THE MANTELPIECE IN ENGLAND, NORMAN?'

'Well, Jane was on holiday in Egypt and saw me in the marketplace with the other extremely well-educated camels and decided that she thought it would broaden my horizons if she brought me back to England.'

'And what does broaden my horizons mean, Norman?'

'Oh, how enchanting; you don't know', he muttered.

'BROADENING ONE'S HORIZONS, MEANS TO UNDERSTAND MORE AND GAIN NEW EXPERIENCES AND KNOWLEDGE.'

'So, am I broadening my horizons too?'

'Yes, indeed you are. Jane will have you travelling around the world with her, believe me.'

Norman's voice quietened and he whispered to me, 'You do know she meant to take me to Peru with her, don't you? Oh, the anguish I felt at being accidentally left behind, when I could have been enjoying the ancient wonders of Peru.'

'Poor you Norman. How awful to be left alone in a cold house.'

'I was very much fine, once I had got over the tremendous disappointment. I found that Jane had left her Encyclopaedia of the World on the coffee table, and as soon as I realised that she had left me here alone, I settled down for the next few weeks to read it. It was fascinating. Oh, how I learnt so much!'

I wasn't too sure what an

EN-SI-CLO-PEE-DEE-YA

was and I didn't want to ask Norman. He seemed so clever and confident.

'Anyway, I have spoken far too much of my intelligence and knowledge.

NOW TELL ME ABOUT YOUR LIFE, YOUNG ALPACA.'

I didn't know where to start. I was a miniature alpaca from a village in Peru. I didn't really know anything of the world, other than how happy my life was and how I had climbed to Machu Picchu and then I had come to England with Jane.

I thought Norman might think I was boring and not very wise, but instead he listened with great enthusiasm to my stories and kept making lots of faces and encouraging me to carry on.

I didn't think I would ever be friends with someone as clever as him, but he loved hearing about my life in Peru and I enjoyed telling him all about it.

HE WANTED ME TO DESCRIBE EVERYTHING IN GREAT DETAIL.

'OH, HOW GLORIOUS, JEFF!

Your tales of Peru have made me feel as though I was there myself, and my disappointment at not going has greatly lessened.'

Norman told me about all the countries he had travelled to with Jane and all the places he wanted to go to.

HE TOLD ME HOW HE MISSED HIS FRIENDS IN EGYPT, VERY MUCH LIKE I MISSED MINE IN PERU.

He confided in me how lonely it had been on the mantelpiece and muttered, 'I'm rather glad you arrived when you did, Jeff.'

As the days passed and we got into our routine of life on the mantelpiece, Norman and I became firm friends. If Jane was in the sitting room during the day we kept very still and quiet. But if she was at work or in another room, we would talk about many different subjects and move around when we needed to. Norman chewed his lips from side to side when he was thinking. He said that is what camels do when they have a lot on their minds. I thought to myself, he must have a lot on his mind because he was *always* chewing.

Sometimes he got cross with me, like when I asked him why camels have humps on their backs.

'MY DEAR BOY, NOW TELL ME WHY *YOU* THINK WE HAVE HUMPS?'

'Well, I'm not sure Norman but I think I heard that you keep water and apples and a first aid kit in there in case of emergencies…'

'UTTERLY RIDICULOUS!'

He stopped me before I could finish and rolled his eyes with annoyance. He then let out a very loud sigh, louder than I had ever heard before.

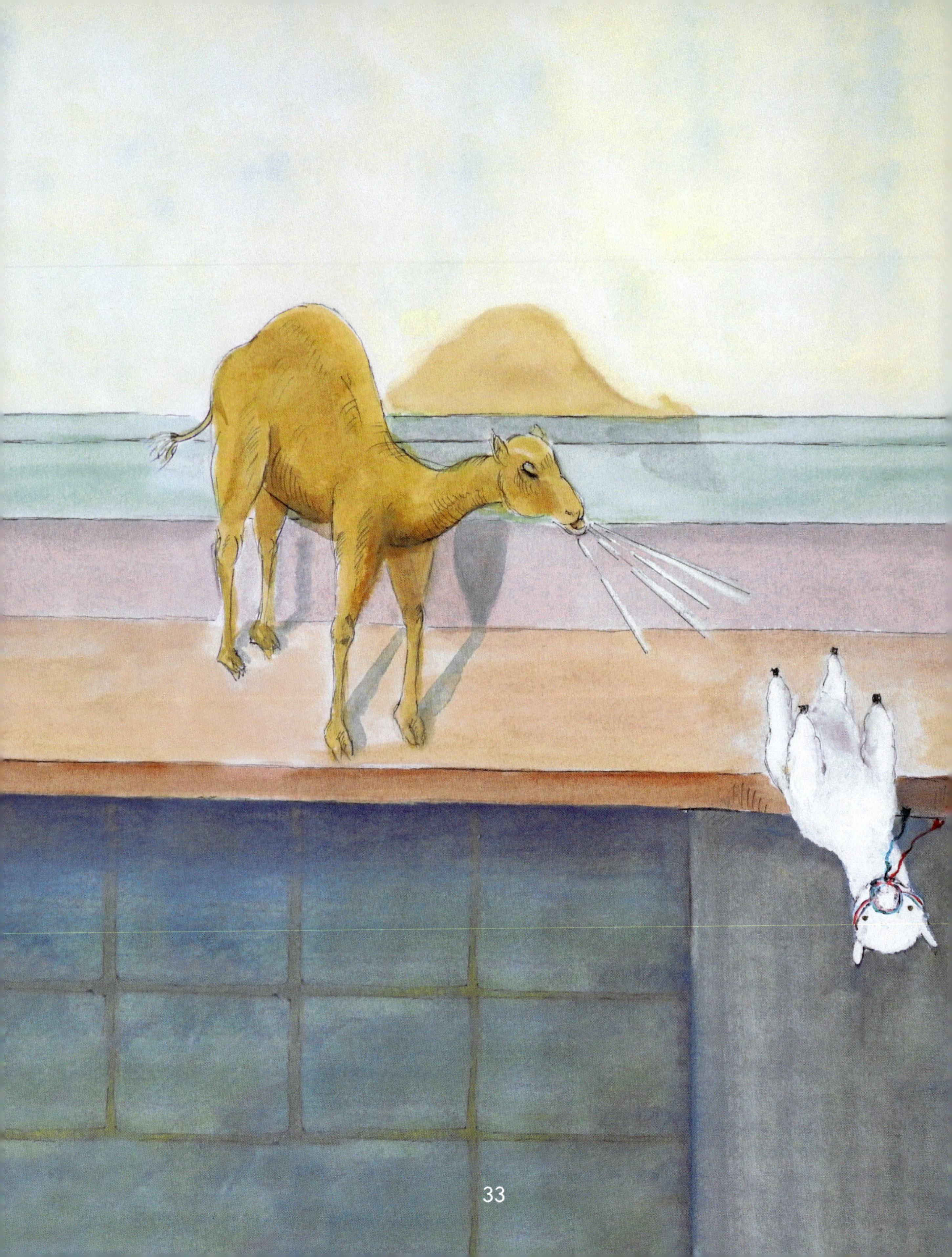

'Jeff, my kind but innocent friend. Our humps contain nothing but fat. So many people think they are full of water, but they are in fact filled with fat. Because we are from the desert, we can go many months without food or water and just use the contents of our humps to keep us nourished. And *that* is why I think camels are one of *the* most exquisite creatures on this earth.'

'OH, OK NORMAN, THANK YOU FOR LETTING ME KNOW THAT.'

Norman let out another very big sigh and then without any warning inhaled a large amount of air. His nostrils started shaking and he then let out the most enormous sneeze I had ever heard. It was so loud and so ferocious it made me jump out of my skin, and I started to wobble on the mantelpiece!

BEFORE I KNEW IT, I COULD FEEL MYSELF FALLING OFF THE EDGE OF THE MANTELPIECE,

rolling through the air and onto the hearth below. It all happened so quickly that I found myself lying on my back with my legs in the air.

I looked up and I could see Norman staring down at me chewing his lips rapidly and with a worried look in his eye.

'MY POOR FRIEND! ARE YOU INJURED?'

'N, n, no Norman, I'm not injured, but I am a little shaken and frightened.'

I tried not to cry as suddenly I felt very alone. I looked round and realised I had fallen onto some black stones.

'Oh, dear boy, you've fallen into the coal bucket. Now get up on your feet and let me see what you look like.'

I rolled over and got onto my feet and looked
up at Norman.

His lip started quivering and I could see he was
trying not to laugh.

'What is it Norman, what are you laughing at?'

'Such amusement', he said quietly, but loudly
enough that I could hear.

'You, my dear boy, look as though you have
fallen down a coal mine. Oh, I must stop
myself from laughing.

THIS REALLY IS THE FUNNIEST THING I HAVE SEEN IN MANY YEARS!'

I looked up at him and I felt a little bit humiliated,
so I turned away to face the door. The last time
I had gone through the doorway was when Jane
brought me back from Peru. It suddenly dawned
on me that there was life beyond the mantelpiece,
and the thought of exploring made my heart
beat a little faster.

Jane told me I must always be brave and
so that is what I must be.

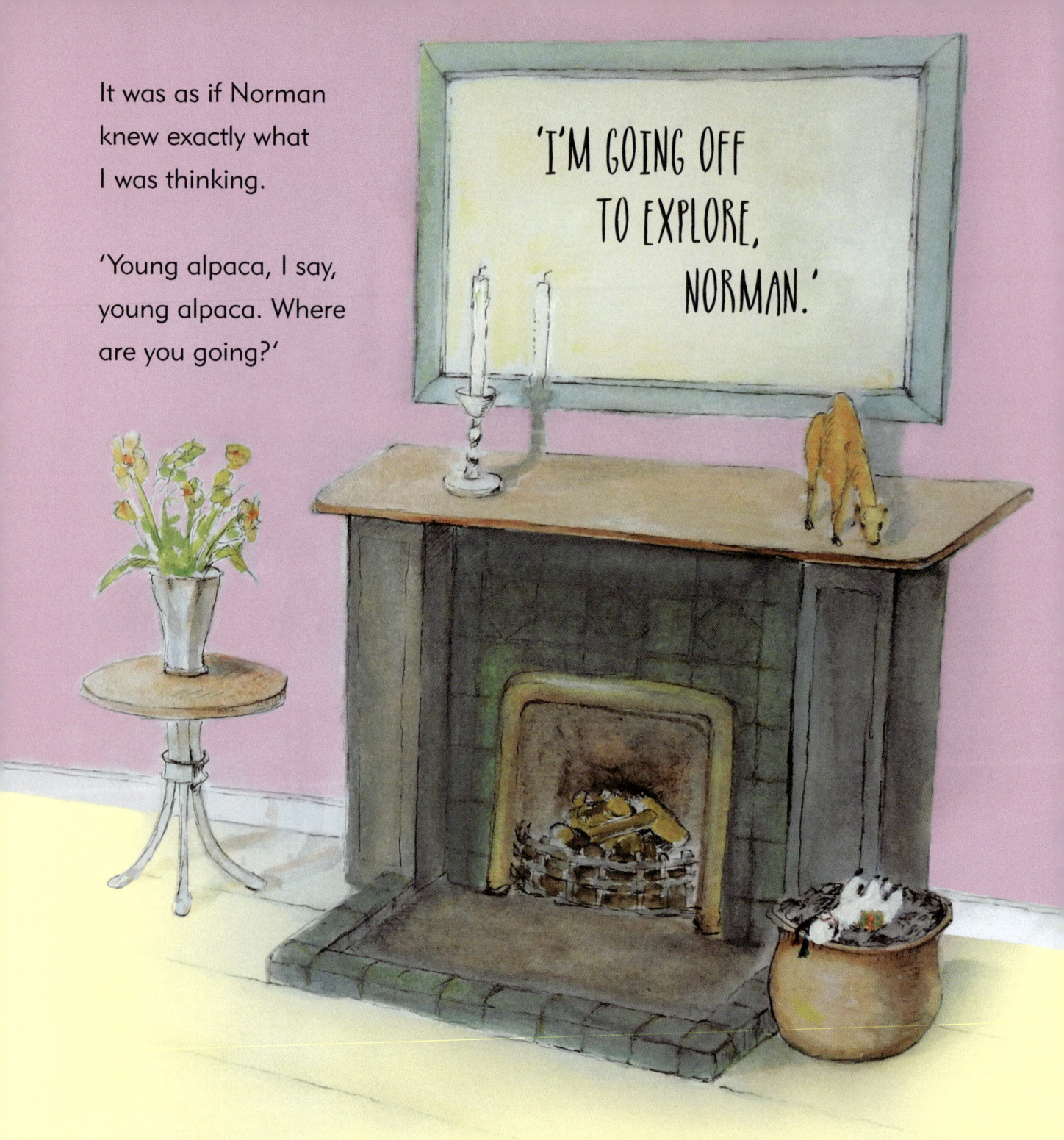

It was as if Norman knew exactly what I was thinking.

'Young alpaca, I say, young alpaca. Where are you going?'

'I'M GOING OFF TO EXPLORE, NORMAN.'

'No. No, don't do that, it's a frightening world out there. Please stay, my dear friend. I will help you get back up here to the mantelpiece and we can enjoy each other's company yet again.'

'I'm upset Norman. I feel silly for falling off the mantelpiece and you laughing at me. I just want to go and see what's out there and see if I can make it back to my village.'

'Jeff, Jeff, my dear boy. I am so sorry. Please be very, very careful.

THERE ARE SOME BIG, SCARY CREATURES OUT THERE.

I heard Jane telling her friend that her next-door neighbour has a dog called a French Bulldog. Jane was laughing as her neighbour had thought she had to speak to it in French. Have you *ever* heard of anything so absurd?!'

He laughed so much, his lips and the hump on his back started to wobble. His amusement about silly people who weren't as clever as him made me feel a little sad. I started to question if a humble alpaca like me was enough for him to have as a friend. Maybe Jane would go back to Egypt, and find a nice intelligent camel friend to keep him company.

'Norman, I have to go. I don't think I belong here.

I'M GOING TO TRY AND FIND MY WAY BACK HOME. BACK HOME TO THE BASKET IN PERU.'

'You are being utterly ridiculous my dear friend. There is no chance on this earth for you to get back to Peru. I know you miss your dear friends and playing together in the village, but believe me, I have been there with my thoughts of how to find my way back to Egypt too.

THIS IS OUR HOME AND WE HAVE TO GET USED TO IT.'

'But I'm going to try, Norman. If I don't try then I won't know, and at least I will be pleased that I have done my best.'

Norman started chewing frantically on his lips and I could see how deep in thought he was.

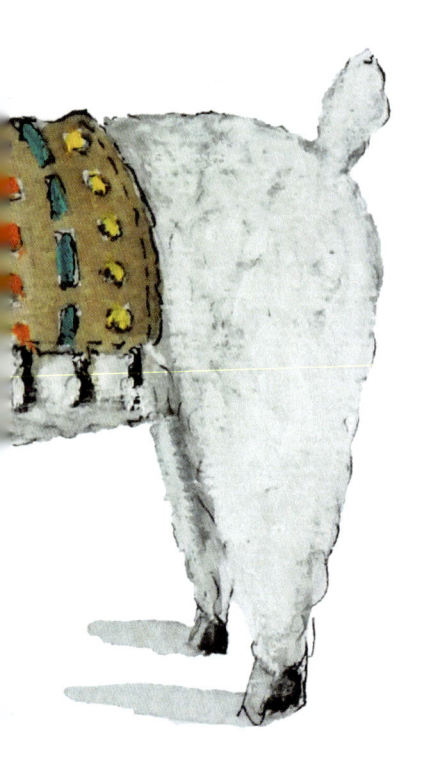

'BRAVE YOUNG ALPACA,
I ADMIRE YOU.

Now, promise me that you will tell me *everything* when you return, won't you?'

'Of course I will, Norman… if I return.' I turned around and looked up at him on the mantelpiece. His head was tilted to one side and I could see his eyes looked very sad.

'Don't be upset, Norman.'

'Upset? Me? I'm not upset. I'm just deep in my thoughts of greatness.' He cleared his throat and gave me a wistful smile. I knew at that moment that he was going to miss me.

'GOODBYE FOR NOW NORMAN. I WILL MISS YOU VERY MUCH.'

'Goodbye, Jeff, my dear friend. Just a gentle reminder that bravery isn't always about putting yourself in danger. Bravery comes in many forms, and I am sure you will discover that during your travels.'

'THANK YOU, NORMAN, YOUR WISE WORDS WILL STAY IN MY HEART FOREVER.'

I shook myself to get rid of the coal dust and turned away from Norman, putting one tiny step in front of the other as I headed towards the sitting room door.

THE DOOR WAS WIDE OPEN, AND WHEN I REACHED IT, I LOOKED DOWN TO SEE A TILED FLOOR

that led to the front door on my right. I had been that way already with Jane, so instead I turned left, past the staircase, and headed to another door. This door was slightly ajar, and I carefully looked through into the room to see what was there. It was a kitchen full of interesting things to look at.

I had never been in a kitchen before, but Norman had told me that this is where people cooked food. I heard a rustling sound and tried to find somewhere to hide.

'OI! 'OI YOU! YEAH, YOU. OOO DO YOU FINK YOU ARE THEN?'

I could feel my heart race and my legs shake as there was nowhere to hide. I looked round to see a big brown mouse, with a very large belly, who was staring right at me. He was wearing a brown waistcoat and carrying a walking cane.

'I'M ALFIE. THAT'S WHAT EVERYONE KNOWS ME AS.'

I felt a little scared, and cowered with fear as he sounded quite gruff.

'Don't worry son, I ain't gonna hurt ya. I'm just interested, that's all. I ain't never met a fing like you before. What are you? You ain't a mouse or rat, are you now?'

HE LOOKED ME UP AND DOWN, SIZING ME UP.

Maybe I had spent too much time with Norman, but suddenly I felt very smart. I put my shoulders back and head up and said,

'MY NAME IS JEFF AND I AM A MINIATURE ALPACA WHO HAS TRAVELLED ALL THE WAY FROM PERU.'

'Poo-roo. Poo where? Never 'erd of it laddy. Is it near Lan-dan?'

'You mean London?'

'YEAH, LAN—DAN.'

'Oh goodness, no. I'm from Peru, which is in South America.'

'Oh, well that's good then matey, cos I'm from Sarf Lan-dan so we got summink in common, ain't we then?'

I wasn't sure if we had yet got *anything* in common, but if I was going to get by in this new world I wasn't quite used to, I had to make friends.

44

'HOW DID YOU ARRIVE IN THIS HOUSE ALFIE, IF YOU'VE COME FROM LONDON?'

'Well, funny you say that son. Jane what lives here was staying in a bed & breakfast in Lan-dan.'

Alfie's voice went very quiet and he started whispering, 'I could smell she 'ad some right treats in 'er bag, she did. I stayed in 'er bedroom, as still as could be, waiting for 'er to drop off into the land of nod.'

'She 'ad these cheese biscuits that were in an 'arf opened packet in her bag. Best biscuits I'd ever 'ad in me life, melt in your mouth proper they did.

I COULDN'T STOP EATING 'EM AN' THEN I SETTLED MESELF DOWN IN 'ER BAG, ALL COSY AN' WARM LIKE!'

'Cor, Jane didn't 'arf snore that night. I started to fink I ain't ever gonna get any sleep meself. Took me ages to drop off, plus me belly was grumbling an' groaning an' making all sorts of terrible noises.'

'I curled up in 'er bag, an' when I finally got off to sleep I slept like a baby mouse in a summer field I did. My belly was full to the brim. I couldn't have 'ad another crumb if I'd tried, an' I felt like a king!'

'Trouble is, I was so full I couldn't move a muscle. It weren't till I got back 'ere that I realised I was no longer in the bed & breakfast but in some other 'ouse miles away. I must've slept through the 'ole journey back 'ere an' Jane 'ad no idea she 'ad even brought me back with 'er! Cor, she would've had a shock if she reached in 'er bag and picked *me* up!'

ALFIE HAD STARTED DRIBBLING AT THE THOUGHT OF THE BISCUITS

and I couldn't stop staring at him as he was reliving such a magical moment in his life.

'Oh, sorry about that son, I've only got a couple of teeth. Makes me dribble a bit, 'specially when I's 'ungry.'

'You probably noticed I ain't got many teeth. Well it's cos I've 'ad so many sweeties an' naughty fings to gobble on over the years.'

'I did notice, Alfie, and it's ok, don't worry about your dribbly mouth.'

I had always been taught to have good manners and to always be kind, even when someone was dribbling when they were thinking about cheese biscuits.

 'Alfie, I also ended up in Jane's bag, but that was because she bought me as a soo-ven-ear when she was on holiday in Peru.'

'And I've decided, I want to go off exploring again and to see if I can find my way back home to my village in Peru. Is there anywhere you recommend, to help me please?'

'Well, I ain't ever 'erd of a 'soo-ven-ear' before an' I ain't too sure where 'Poo-roo' is in the world but either way son, you've come to the right place.

I KNOWS ALL THE BEST PLACES FOR SIGHTSEEING ROUND 'ERE.'

Alfie was keen to take me on a tour of the kitchen, and apparently his favourite place in the whole world was under the fridge. According to him there was a great selection of food scraps you could find there, everything from cheese slithers to mouldy grapes. Alfie said Jane would kick the scraps under the fridge to save her having to hoover them up.

'SHE'S GOOD LIKE THAT IS OUR JANE.'

Alfie showed me the pantry. 'You gotta be careful if you 'ave anything out of 'ere. You can't just take a few bites from a biscuit. You've gotta eat the 'ole blinkin' biscuit else otherwise Jane will know that there's been mice in 'ere an' that is the last fing on this earth what we want to 'appen, else we've all gotta find a new 'ome.'

'ALL? WHAT DO YOU MEAN ALL?'

'Well, I don't live 'ere on me own son, do I? Oh no, I couldn't imagine for one moment being a solitary mouse, I've got far too much to say for meself. I met me wife, Betty, in this 'ouse 'ere. She's a seaside mouse born an' bred, so she is. She's the kindest mouse what you will ever meet. We've got eight children, five girls an' three boys, all little dazzlers they are, bright as buttons an' sweet as you can imagine.'

'OH, HOW WONDERFUL ALFIE TO HAVE EIGHT CHILDREN AND A WIFE.

HOW CHARMING AND LOVELY!'

Alfie beamed with delight. 'Well, fank you very much sonny. Ain't you just the nicest young chap! Never met a tiny alpaca before but ain't you just made my day.'

'Thank you, Alfie. I'm so grateful for you showing me around the kitchen. It's been very exciting. I just wondered if you know anything about the outside of the house and where might be somewhere interesting to go to that might help me get back home?'

'Oh, outside? What you wants is to go out in the big world, laddy? Now are you sure about this?'

'Yes, I'm certain, Alfie. Please let me know where I can go to explore and get back to Peru.'

Alfie went very, very quiet. 'You know that big camel, Norman, what sits on the mantelpiece? Well, he tried to get 'ome to his place in Egypt a couple of years ago. He'd 'erd that one of the neighbours was going on 'oliday there an' the silly old fing fort he could sneak into their suitcase without 'em knowing!'

'Rumour 'as it that Mr Mee-Yowzer, the grey cat from three doors down, 'ad been lurking under the neighbour's 'edge an' he spotted Norman making his way through the undergrowth. Played with him for a while, tossed 'im up in the air he did, then carried 'im off an' left 'im on a branch up a pear tree in next door's garden. Five nights he was stuck in that tree for, can you imagine?'

'Poor old boy, it was only cos it was such a windy night that he fell out the tree; battered an' bruised he was. An' after sitting in the sun for a few days he was eventually reunited with Jane.

FINK IT PROPERLY SHOOK 'IM TO THE CORE.'

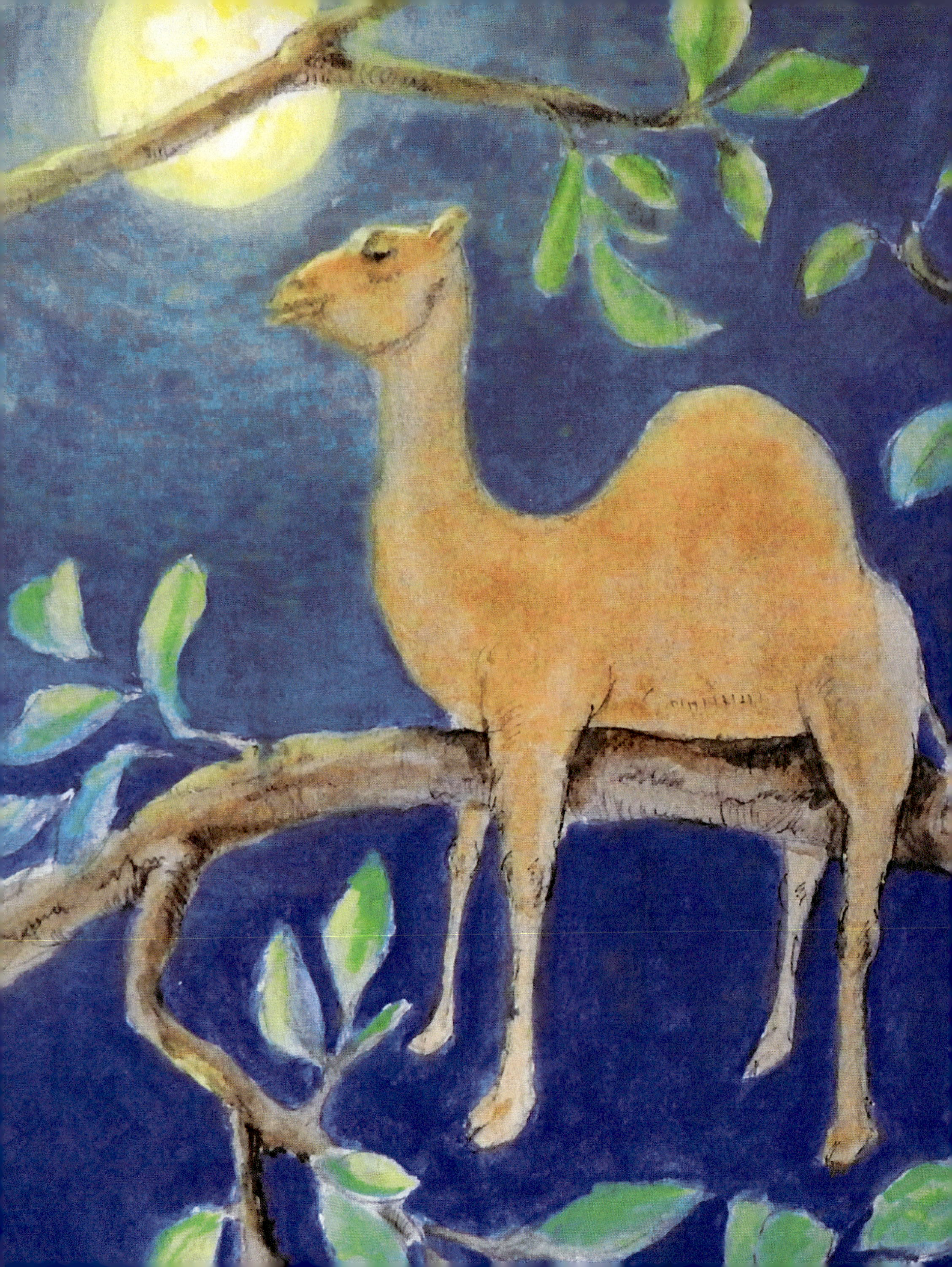

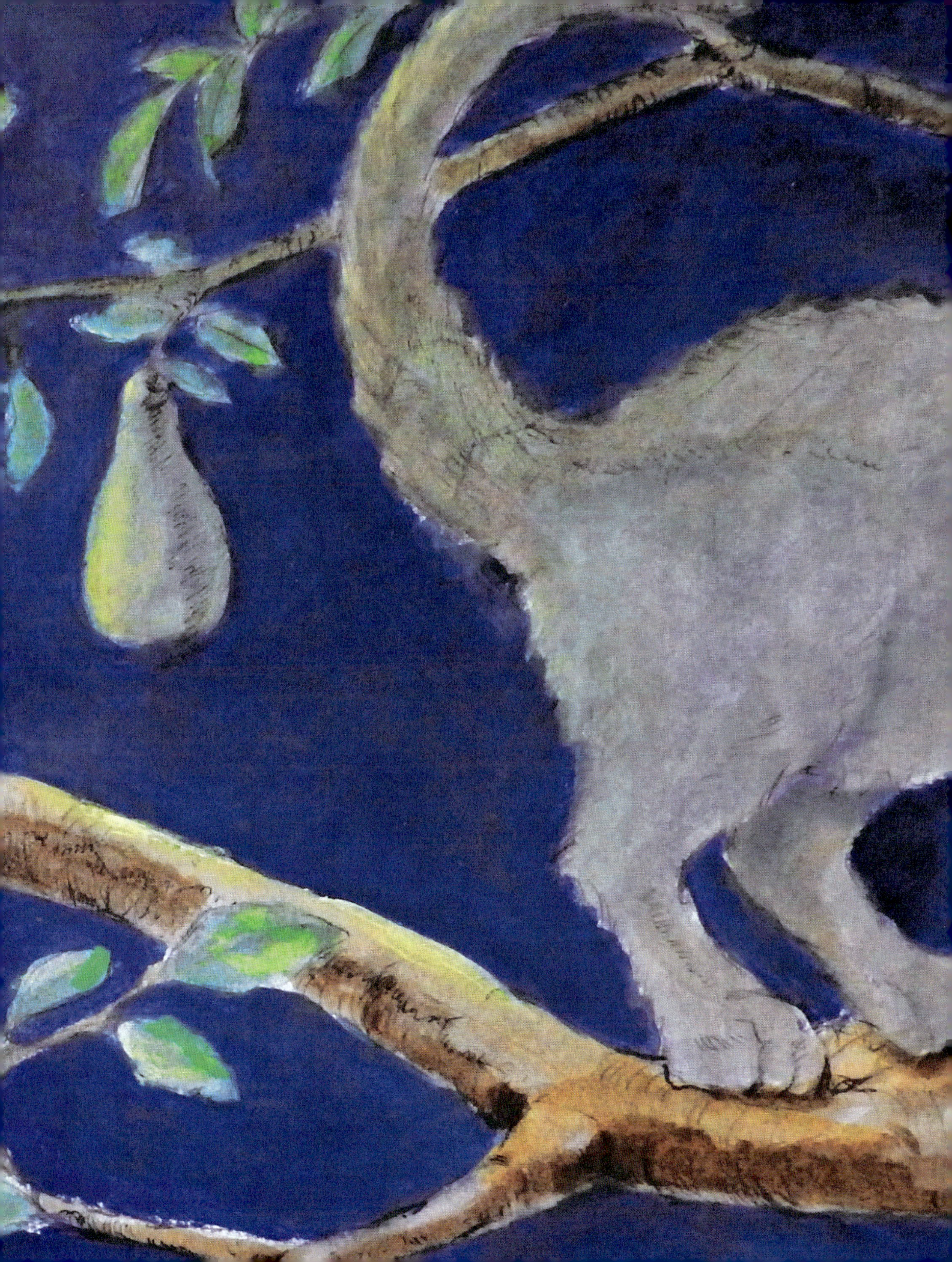

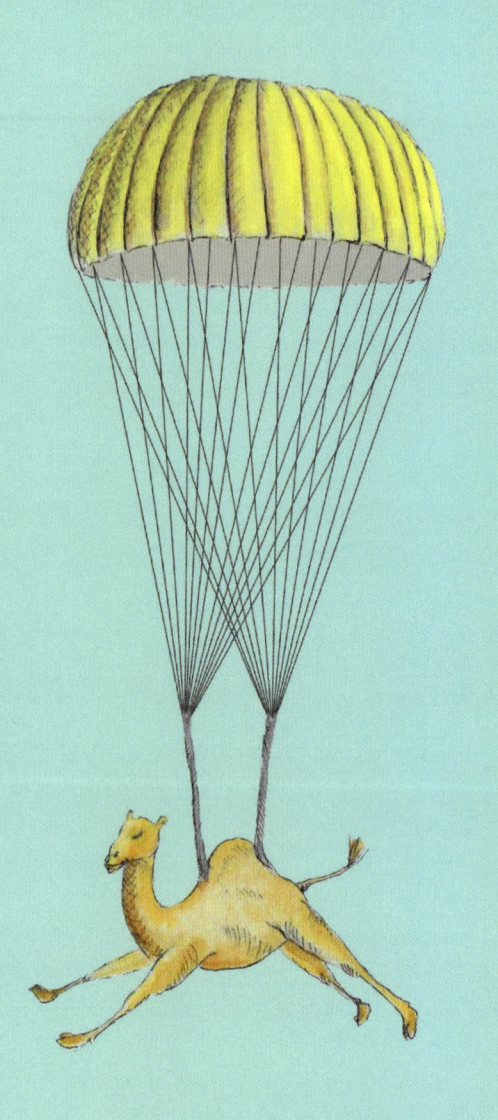

'Oh my word Alfie, how awful for poor Norman. I know he warned me about the dangers of the outside but I had no idea he had been through such a frightening experience.'

'I fink it's why he's a bit of a difficult old fing. For all his bravado that camel 'as an 'art of gold he does. I saw 'im when Jane brought 'im back in the 'ouse. I'll never forget he 'ad this worried old look to his face. He saw me looking out from under the pantry door an' I grinned at 'im, give 'im a wave to welcome 'im back. He weren't too impressed when I said to 'im,

"IT'S A SHAME YOU AIN'T GOT A PARACHUTE IN THAT HUMP OF YOURS, SON!"

'He just rolled his eyes at me but I was so glad that old boy got back 'ome safe that day.'

It made me shudder to think of Mr Mee-Yowzer and how he had been watching poor Norman, waiting to pounce on him.

'I know you're curious about the world son, but you've already come from some place a million miles away, whatcha call it again? Poo-roo, weren't it?'

'Err, erm, something like that Alfie.'

'Well, if you're sure laddy, I'll take you outside an' show you what it's all about an' see if we can get you back to Poo-roo.'

Alfie was nice to me and I felt humbled by his kindness.

He clapped his hands and said,

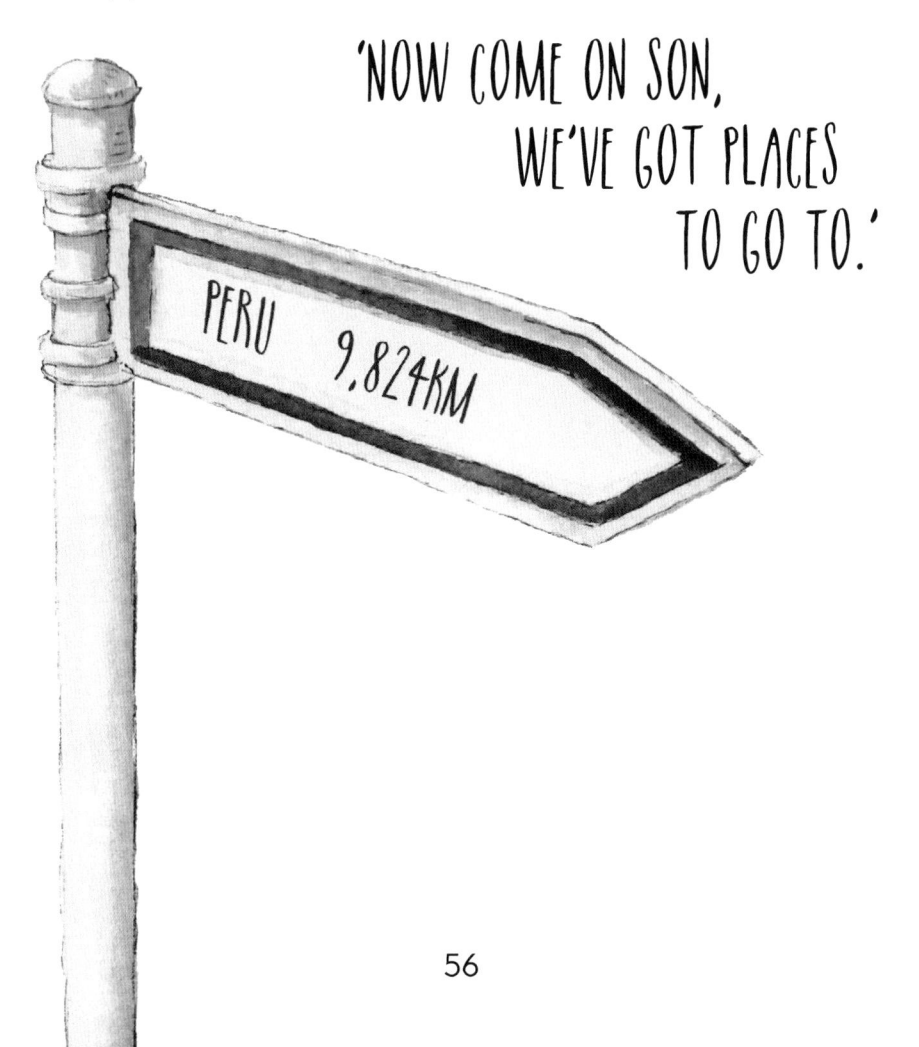

'NOW COME ON SON, WE'VE GOT PLACES TO GO TO.'

PERU   9,824KM

I smiled back at Alfie and thanked him for helping me. I started wondering how on earth we were going to get out of the house and into the garden. But Alfie was on a mission and I had no time to ask questions. We turned around from the kitchen and made a dash for the hallway and towards the front door.

'WHERE ARE WE GOING, ALFIE?'

'We're 'eadin for the letterbox, son.'

Suddenly I realised that Jane had a very funny old-fashioned letterbox that was near the bottom of her front door.

Alfie shouted out, 'They don't make 'em like this anymore, laddy!'

With the help of his walking cane, Alfie pushed open the letterbox and made a gap big enough for us both to get out.

I COULD SMELL THE FRESH SALTY SEA AIR AND I PAUSED FOR A MOMENT TO INHALE IT.

'We need to get into the
back garden, son. Keep to the
side of the house. It's safer.'

I followed Alfie as he carefully ran past some
flowerpots and alongside the brickwork of the
house. He squeezed underneath a wooden fence
and, before I knew it, we were in the back garden
where there was a lawn and flower beds.

I could just make out the pear tree next door,
where poor Norman had got stuck for those five
long days and nights.

The garden was pretty, and the grass was soft but a little bit damp.

I PAUSED TO SMELL SOME BEAUTIFUL, SWEET FLOWERS.

ALFIE POINTED OUT THAT THE BEST FLOWERS IN THE GARDEN WERE THE SUNFLOWERS.

Even though they were tall he told me that he could get handfuls of seeds from them whenever he pleased. He said it was a long climb up to the top of the sunflowers but he would poke at the seeds with his walking cane until they dropped to the ground, where he would collect them. He was such a clever mouse, full of wise ideas. We both stood back to admire the beautiful flowers.

Suddenly, Alfie froze and became as still as a statue. He had a serious look on his face.

'Jeff, you see that garden shed over there?'

He pointed to the far right of the garden, which seemed like a very long way away.

'YES, I CAN SEE IT ALFIE. WHY?'

'WE'VE 'GOTTA MAKE A RUN FOR IT, SON.

Don't ask any questions. Just follow me an' run as fast as you can.'

Alfie could run very, very fast. At times I found it hard to keep up with him. He knew I wasn't as fast as him but he kept looking over his shoulder to see that I was still following.

I could hear heavy breathing right on our tails, getting closer and closer.

'UNDER 'ERE SON, QUICK!'

Alfie shot underneath the shed and shouted, 'Grab the cane!'

He held his walking cane out for me, which I grabbed with my mouth. He then helped to haul me underneath the shed and I just managed to squeeze in next to him.

We were both gasping for air and I found it hard to understand what had just happened.

'YOU ALRIGHT, SON?'

'I, I think so Alfie.'

The next thing we knew a big grey paw was feeling around underneath the shed trying to reach us. It clipped my leg and made me flinch.

'Move further back', Alfie called out to me.

I knew at once that this was Mr Mee-Yowzer, the cat who had taken poor Norman off.

'DON'T WORRY LADDY, HE CAN'T GET UNDER 'ERE'.

'Are you sure Alfie?'

'There's one fing I knows all about, an' that is Mr Mee-Yowzer. He's always 'ad 'is eye on me, an' I've always 'ad a lot of fun outwittin' 'im. He likes to fink he's clued up but he ain't ever dealt with a streetwise mouse like me before.'

Of all the things that had happened, from leaving the basket in Peru, to flying on an aeroplane, to falling off the mantelpiece, this was the most frightening so far.

Alfie must have noticed I looked worried as he started reassuring me with his tales of outwitting Mr Mee-Yowzer, as we watched his paw swiping back and forth at us. I had never met a cat before, but he was hissing at us and seemed very irritated.

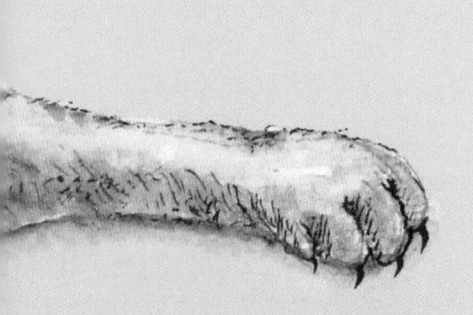

'He always gets like this when he's bored. He won't stay 'ere forever. We can stay 'ere for hours if we need to. I've got the patience of a saint, me.'

Alfie made me feel very protected. He started telling me all about the close shaves he had experienced with Mr Mee-Yowzer. He was so funny, making me laugh with his stories of great escapes!

'You want some raisins, son?'

Alfie reached into the inside pocket of his waistcoat and dug out a raisin, which he broke in half for us to share.

'You've always gotta keep supplies on you, son, bit like our friend Norman wiv that old 'ump of 'is.'

I thought back to Norman on the mantelpiece and how long he had waited for a friend to keep him company. He could be a bit of a grumpy camel at times, but I missed him and I knew he would be missing me too. I thought about his wise words about bravery and how right he had been.

'How long do you think it will be before Mr Mee-Yowzer goes home, Alfie?'

'HE WON'T BE MUCH LONGER NOW. HE KNOWS I'M FAR TOO CLEVER FOR 'IM.'

'Go on away with you matey, you've 'ad your fun, now clear off!' Alfie waved his stick at Mr Mee-Yowzer as he tried shooing him away.

'Thank goodness you're here Alfie. I don't know what I would have done without you.'

'You'd 'ave ended up sat in the pear tree for days just like our Norman did, I imagine.'

I FELT SO GRATEFUL FOR MY COURAGEOUS FRIEND LOOKING OUT FOR ME.

'Now son, I'm not too sure what Norman's told you but she's an adventurous gal is our Jane. You know she'll be takin' you an' Norman on all sorts of travels, don't you?'

'Will she really, Alfie? Norman was saying he had been to lots of countries with Jane.'

'Yeah, she'll take the two of you everywhere, believe me. So, it probably ain't really worth you chancin' your luck on your own in the big wide world. You'll 'ave someone 'oo will look after you an' give you a lifetime of adventures. Plus, you'll 'ave your very own tour guide to keep you company in Norman. He knows everything an' anything about the world, he does.'

I looked at Alfie and knew he was right.

THIS WHOLE EXPERIENCE HAD MADE ME REALISE THAT I HAD THE KINDEST OF FRIENDS IN ALFIE AND NORMAN.

I knew one day I would see my friends in Peru again, but for now this was most definitely my home and I felt my heart fill with happiness.

Alfie grinned at me.

'Nice, weren't it, that raisin? You can't make decisions on an empty stomach son, and I could see you was 'ungry.'

'It was a lovely raisin Alfie, thank you.'

'I think I might have seen enough of the garden. Would it be alright to go back home to the house, once Mr Mee-Yowzer has moved on?'

'You bet, son. I didn't like to say, but I noticed Jane 'ad left out some more raisins from when she was baking a cake yesterday. They'll do me, Betty and the children nicely for our dinner.'

'THANK YOU, ALFIE. YOU HAVE BEEN SO KIND TO ME.'

'Oh laddy, ain't you just got the nicest of manners. Always know, son, I'm 'ere if you ever needs me.'

All of a sudden Alfie jumped up and said, 'Right, he's gone, time for us to make a move an' get ourselves 'ome, son!'

We peered out from the shed and checked every direction for Mr Mee-Yowzer before making a run for it. Alfie hid behind some dandelion leaves as I stayed under the shed.

'STAY CLOSE TO ME, LADDY!'

I ran after Alfie as he darted back towards the house, following the same route as before. We shot back under the garden fence, past the brickwork and across to the front door. All the time we were running I hoped that Mr Mee-Yowzer wouldn't suddenly appear.

Alfie held open the letterbox with his cane and we climbed back into the hallway of the house.

'WE MADE IT SON!'

Alfie beamed, and he seemed very proud of himself as we headed back towards the sitting room. It was there that we said our temporary goodbyes to one another. We knew we would see each other again soon, and I thanked him yet again for his generosity and kindness.

Alfie winked at me and said, 'If you ever see any of them cheese biscuits on your travels, put one on your saddle for me, laddy!'

'I PROMISE I WILL, ALFIE.'

And with those parting words, Alfie wandered off back to the kitchen to enjoy his well-earned dinner of raisins, and any other things he had collected along the way, with his wife and family.

I had just started making my way into the sitting room when I heard a key turn in the lock of the front door. I gasped as I realised it was Jane coming back home from work.

Norman spotted me in the doorway and called out,

'STAY STILL, YOUNG ALPACA,
AND DROP ONTO YOUR SIDE.'

I did just that and I heard Jane's footsteps getting closer and closer and closer. She paused for a second and looked at me, very puzzled.

'JEFF! WHAT *ARE* YOU DOING DOWN THERE? YOU POOR THING!

The wind must have blown you over when I opened the window upstairs this morning.'

She gently picked me up and put me next to Norman on the mantelpiece.

'There you go boys, you're back together again, safe and sound.' Jane smiled at us both before turning around and walking off in the direction of the kitchen.

I turned to Norman, and his face looked so soft and kind. I whispered to him, 'I have so much to tell you.'

'I KNOW YOU DO, YOUNG ALPACA. I'VE MISSED YOU VERY MUCH. IT'S BEEN SO LONELY WITHOUT YOU.'

'I've missed you too, Norman.'

'Now, before you tell me all about the excitement of the great outdoors, young alpaca, I have a question. Do you think you will be happy living here on the mantelpiece, going on adventures with Jane and a silly old camel like myself?'

'THERE IS NOWHERE I WOULD RATHER BE, NORMAN, THAN HERE WITH YOU, MY BEST FRIEND, AND TRAVELLING THE WORLD TOGETHER.'

Norman blushed a little bit and his kind face showed how happy he was that I was safely back.

'I'M SO GLAD TO BE HOME, NORMAN'

'Not as happy as I am, my dear, dear friend. We have so much to look forward to.'

I smiled at Norman and he smiled back. Of all the changes I had experienced, there was one thing I was certain of. Whatever happened and wherever we went in the world...

NORMAN AND I WOULD ALWAYS
BE THE BEST OF FRIENDS.

ACKNOWLEDGEMENTS

For James, my Ma and Pa (Marion and Steve Bartlett) and all the Kinsley Family. With love, always.

Our grateful thanks go to Phil Appleby for proofreading and editing our book and to Alice Kinsley, for her endless patience and creativity in formatting our book for publishing. We couldn't have done this without you both.

Text and Illustrations
© Sophie Louise Kinsley
and Paul W. Kinsley 2020.

No part of this publication can be reproduced without the written consent of the author and illustrator.

Printed in Poland
by Amazon Fulfillment
Poland Sp. z o.o., Wrocław